WHAT SAITH THE

SCRIPTURE?

Inward Holiness
Outward Holiness
Separation From the World

DEDICATION

I dedicate this book to the next generation — the youth of tomorrow. May they ask for the old paths, where is the good way, and walk therein. (Jeremiah 6:16)

SPECIAL THANKS

To Tim and Teresa Wodoslawsky for your help compiling this booklet.

To Richard Cantu for the front cover image.

To Aaron Marquez of AMARQUEZ.DESIGN for the cover design.

To Sandy Kilby for compiling my notes several years ago on *What Saith The Scripture? Concerning Inward and Outward Holiness*.

Thank you to the following proofreaders and editors: Juanita Barnes, Natalia Aguilar, Story Wodoslawsky, and Valena Wodoslawsky.

Thank you to the ministers who reviewed the manuscript: Pastor Timothy Lackey, Pastor Larry Montano and Elder Galen Gregg.

INTRODUCTION

The purpose of this writing is to provide seed thoughts. It is simple points and scriptures to consider regarding inward and outward holiness and separation from the world. Holiness never ends. There is more to it than this booklet. May we take these principles and apply them to our lives.

WHAT SAITH THE SCRIPTURE?

In Romans 4:3 we find these four words, "What saith the scripture?" In Galatians 4:30 we find these same four words, "What saith the scripture?" The word scripture means a document holy written, sacred writings.

Now, when an automobile is manufactured, the manufacturer puts a book inside the automobile called the OWNER'S MANUAL. That book tells us how it is supposed to operate, what it can do and what it cannot do. It tells us how to keep it in good, working condition and how to keep it clean on the inside and the outside. If something goes wrong, it tells us how to fix it. If we follow the owner's manual, the value and life of that automobile is greatly improved.

Genesis 1:27 So God created man in his own image, in the image of God created he him; male and female created he them.

The Bible, the Word of God, is our owner's manual. The scriptures that are given to us within the pages of this book tell us all about our God and how we are to live our lives to please him. We must follow the owner's manual, the Bible. We are admonished to search the scriptures.

John 5:39 Search the scriptures; for in them ye think ye have eternal life: and they are they which testify of me.

Acts 17:11 These were more noble than those in Thessalonica, in that they received the word with all readiness of mind, and searched the scriptures daily, whether those things were so.

Acts 17:2 And Paul, as his manner was, went in unto them, and three sabbath days <u>reasoned with them out of the scriptures</u>,

Acts 18:24 And a certain Jew named Apollos, born at Alexandria, an eloquent man, and <u>mighty in the scriptures</u>, came to Ephesus.

Romans 1:2 Which he had promised afore by his prophets in the <u>holy scriptures</u>,

II Timothy 3:15 And that <u>from a child thou hast known the holy scriptures</u>, which are able to make thee wise unto salvation through faith which is in Christ Jesus.

John 2:22 When therefore he was risen from the dead, his disciples remembered that he had said this unto them; and <u>they believed the scripture</u>, and the word which Jesus had said.

Luke 24:32, 45 And they said one to another, Did not our heart burn within us, while he talked with us by the way, and while <u>he opened to us the scriptures</u>?... Then opened he their understanding, that <u>they might understand the scriptures,</u>

II Timothy 3:16, 17 <u>All scripture is given by inspiration of God,</u> and is profitable for doctrine, for reproof, for correction, for instruction in righteousness: That the man of God may be perfect, throughly furnished unto all good works.

WHAT SAITH THE SCRIPTURE?
Know the Word of God

Isaiah 40:8 The grass withereth, the flower fadeth: but <u>the word of our God shall stand for ever.</u>

Mathew 4:4 But he answered and said, It is written, Man shall not live by bread alone, but <u>by every word that proceedeth out of the mouth of God.</u>

Colossians 3:16 <u>Let the word of Christ dwell in you richly in all wisdom;</u> teaching and admonishing one another in psalms and hymns and spiritual songs, singing with grace in your hearts to the Lord.

John 8:31 Then said Jesus to those Jews which believed on him, <u>If ye continue in my word, then are ye my disciples indeed;</u>

Isaiah 66:2 For all those things hath mine hand made, and all those things have been, saith the LORD: but to this man will I look, even to him that is poor and of a contrite spirit, and <u>trembleth at my word.</u>

Jesus said in Matthew 22:29, "<u>Ye do err, not knowing the scriptures.</u>" We need to know the scriptures, which are the Word of God. The song says, "The good ol' Bible is right. Hallelujah to the Lamb!" Oh! ...and while I am thinking about it, let's stick with the good old King James Version Bible!

II Timothy 4:2 <u>Preach the word</u>; be instant in season, out of season; reprove, rebuke, exhort with all longsuffering and doctrine.

Preach the Word!

WHAT SAITH THE SCRIPTURE?
Concerning Holiness

First, we must ask ourselves, "What is holiness?" According to the Hebrew translation, *holiness* means "consecrated, dedicated, clean or to sanctify one's self wholly." The Greek translation defines *holiness* as "modest, pure and set apart." The word *holy* or *holiness* is found in the scriptures over 500 times.

Psalms 97:12 Rejoice in the LORD, ye righteous; and give thanks at <u>the remembrance of his holiness.</u>

Psalms 47:8 God reigneth over the heathen: God sitteth upon <u>the throne of his holiness.</u>

II Corinthians 7:1 Having therefore these promises, dearly beloved, let us cleanse ourselves from all filthiness of the flesh and spirit, <u>perfecting holiness in the fear of God.</u>

Ephesians 4:24 And that ye put on the new man, which after <u>God is created in righteousness and true holiness.</u>

Hebrews 12:14 <u>Follow peace with all men, and holiness</u>, without which no man shall see the Lord:

I Peter 2:9 But ye are a chosen generation, a royal priesthood, <u>an holy nation, a peculiar people</u>; that ye should shew forth the praises of him who hath called you out of darkness into his marvelous light:

Leviticus 10:10 <u>And that ye may put difference between holy and unholy, and between unclean and clean;</u>

Leviticus 20:7 Sanctify yourselves therefore, and <u>be ye holy: for I am the LORD your God.</u>

Romans 12:1 I beseech you therefore, brethren, by the mercies of God, that <u>ye present your bodies a living sacrifice, holy, acceptable unto God, which is your reasonable service.</u>

Ephesians 5:27 That he might present it to himself a glorious church, not having spot, or wrinkle, or any such thing; but that <u>it should be holy and without blemish.</u>

WHAT SAITH THE SCRIPTURE?
Why Holiness?

Psalms 99:9 Exalt the LORD our God, and worship at his holy hill; <u>for the LORD our God is holy.</u>

Leviticus 19:2 Speak unto all the congregation of the children of Israel, and say unto them, <u>Ye shall be holy: for I the LORD your God am holy.</u>

2 Corinthians 5:20 Now then we are ambassadors for Christ…

Our God is holy. He expects His people to be holy. We as Christians are representatives of God's holiness in the world today. We are His ambassadors.

WHAT SAITH THE SCRIPTURE?
Concerning Inward Holiness

Holiness starts on the inside.

Matthew 23:27, 28 Woe unto you, scribes and Pharisees, hypocrites! for ye are like unto whited sepulchres, which indeed appear beautiful outward, <u>but are within full of dead men's bones, and of all uncleanness.</u> Even so ye also outwardly appear righteous unto men, <u>but within ye are full of hypocrisy and iniquity.</u>

Psalms 19:14 <u>Let the words of my mouth, and the meditation of my heart, be acceptable in thy sight,</u> O LORD, my strength, and my redeemer.

Psalms 51:10 <u>Create in me a clean heart, O God; and renew a right spirit within me.</u>

Matthew 5:8 Blessed are the <u>pure in heart:</u> for they shall see God.

Pure means "clean, clear, free from foreign matter, faultless, innocent, guiltless." We can NOT have a heart full of deceit, pride, evil thoughts, hatred, strife, envy, murder, lies, rebellion, adultery, fornication, pornography and still have inward holiness.

If we are to be holy as He is holy, then our hearts must be free from pride, deceit, hate, strife, jealousy, murder, lying, heresies, drunkenness, bad attitudes, and rebellion. The Bible says that they which do such things shall not inherit the kingdom of God.

We also read in Titus 2:11, 12, "For the grace of God that bringeth salvation hath appeared to all men, teaching us that denying ungodliness and worldly lusts, we should live soberly, righteously, and godly, in this present world." Holiness is more than just a dress code. Holiness is a work that has its beginning in the heart. That is why the Bible teaches we must be born of the water and of the Spirit. Before we can be holy as God would have us to be, we must be filled with the Holy Ghost. We cannot live holy without His Holy Spirit in our hearts.

To be pure in heart we must ask ourselves, "What kind of books do we read?" We cannot read lustful or pornographic material, or love and romance novels and keep holiness in our hearts. The apostle Paul said in the book of Philippians, "...whatsoever things are pure, ...if there be any virtue, ...think on these things." We must watch what we read, for it is true, we become what we read.

Not only must we watch what we read, but also what we look at. Thank God that there are people in the land, God's church, that still do not allow television or unfiltered internet in the home or heart. Again, to be pure we must ask ourselves, "What about television, movies, internet, etc.?" For us to be the holy people that God wants us to be, we must have the victory over watching any form of ungodly material. Any form of Hollywood is not of God. Oh God, wash our eyes of the evils of Hollywood. What are we viewing on the internet? What type of ungodly things do we see? What are we downloading on our phones? What are we hiding? What type of secret sins are keeping us from being pure?

Let's not forget to ask ourselves, "What are we listening to?" We must be careful what we lend our ear to. We cannot allow our ears to be filled with the "smutty jokes" and "off-colored talk" of the world. Somehow, these things make their way into our hearts, and thereby, we become defiled. We need to thank God for the Holy Ghost that can guard our hearts and keep us pure and holy within.

The Apostle Paul said in Ephesians 5:18-19, "...be filled with the Spirit; Speaking to yourselves in psalms and hymns and spiritual songs, singing and making melody in your heart to the Lord." Country western, bluegrass, disco, mellow love songs, mood music, soul music and so-called rap music, etc., has no place in the heart of a child of God. This would also include "gospel rock" which is filtering through from recordings of our own Apostolic people. Let's keep our songs spiritual and our hearts clean.

Galatians 5:19-21 Now the works of the flesh are manifest, which are these; Adultery, fornication, uncleanness, lasciviousness, idolatry, witchcraft, hatred, variance, emulations, wrath, strife, seditions, heresies, envyings, murders, drunkenness, revellings, <u>and such like:</u> of the which I tell you before, as I have also told you in time past, that they which do such things shall not inherit the kingdom of God.

The works of the flesh which are manifest are these:

- ADULTERY – sexual relations with the spouse of another.

- FORNICATION – all unlawful sexual relations.

- UNCLEANNESS – whatever is opposite of purity, including sodomy, homosexuality, incest and all other forms of sexual perversion.

- LASCIVIOUSNESS – lustful, filthy. Anything promoting or partaking of that which tends to produce lewd emotions or to foster sexual sin and lust, such as pornography. What are we accessing on the internet? What are we accessing on our phones?

- IDOLATRY – image worship, which also includes anything on which affections are passionately set. For example: sports teams, sports heroes, celebrities or video games.

- WITCHCRAFT – sorcery or the practice of dealing with evil spirits, casting spells, and using charms. Anything magical.

- HATRED – bitter dislike or malice. An ill-will against anyone, to hold grudges or to be angry at someone.

- VARIANCE – causing dissension, discord, quarrelling or debating and disputes.

- EMULATIONS – seeking to surpass and outdo others; having jealousy or striving to excel at the expense of another.

- STRIFE – causing contention. In Proverbs 6, it tells us that there are seven things which God hates, and one of them is "...he that soweth discord among the brethren."

Proverbs 6:16-19 These six things doth the LORD hate: yea, seven are an abomination unto him: A proud look, a lying tongue, and hands that shed innocent blood, An heart that deviseth wicked imaginations, feet that be swift in running to mischief, A false witness that speaketh lies, and he that soweth discord among brethren.

- SEDITIONS – division and stirring up strife.

- HERESIES – anything that is not sound doctrine.

- ENVYINGS – jealousy when good comes to another.
- MURDERS – to kill, to spoil, or to mar the happiness of another or to hate.
- DRUNKENNESS – living intoxicated; a slave to drinking.
- REVELLINGS – party spirit, feasting, obscene music or pleasures.
- <u>AND SUCH LIKE</u>

Notice in verse 21, after it names all these things, then it states, "<u>and such like</u>." Remember the words "such like." Those words can cover a lot of things that we have in this day that Paul did not have in his day. For example, drug abuse of both illegal drugs and prescription drugs.

We may dress like and look like a Pentecostal, but what is going on in our hearts? Things within, such as lying, prayerlessness, pride, a gossiping tongue, a trouble-making spirit, rebellion, an effeminate spirit in a man, and a masculine spirit in a woman are dangerous. Jesus was concerned about what goes on in the inside.

WHAT SAITH THE SCRIPTURE?
Concerning Secret Faults

Psalms 19:12-14 Who can understand his errors? cleanse thou me from secret faults. Keep back thy servant also from presumptuous sins; let them not have dominion over me: then shall I be upright, and I shall be innocent from the great transgression. Let the words of my mouth, and the meditation of my heart, be acceptable in thy sight, O LORD, my strength, and my redeemer.

Presumptuous sins are sins that are willful, deliberate, arrogant, proud, bold, daring, or "in your face." Those who commit such will soon be hardened through the deceitfulness of sin. In Hebrews 3:13, "But exhort one another daily, while it is called today; lest any of you be hardened through the deceitfulness of sin." Referring to Psalms 19:14 mentioned above, David is saying, let my words and my thoughts be pleasing to you, Lord.

What is going on inside of us, in our hearts, in our minds, in our soul and in our spirit? An old song says,

"How about your heart, is it right with God?
That's the thing that counts today.
Is it black by sin, is it pure within?
Could we ask Christ in to stay?
People often see us as we are outside,
Jesus really knows us for He sees inside.
How about your heart, is it right with God?
That's the thing that counts today."

Whatever is in our heart that is not right, we must deal with it. We need to deal with it now! Romans 2:4 teaches the goodness of God leads us to repentance.

Where are our thoughts taking us? Where have we been? Where are we? Where are we going?

We Pentecostals are known for our outward holiness, and we do not want to take away from that. When our inward holiness is taken care of, our outward holiness will be right. We can look right on the outside and be very wrong in our heart. The scripture says in I Samuel 16:7, "...the LORD seeth not as man seeth; for man looketh on the outward appearance, but the LORD looketh on the heart." Holiness must be a heart experience. <u>The Bible says in II Corinthians 5:12 that there are people, "...which glory in appearance, and not in</u>

heart." They pride themselves on outward appearances, but the heart is not right. Remember, Matthew 5:8 says, "Blessed are the pure in heart: for they shall see God."

Search me, O God, and know my heart today,
Try me, O Savior know my thoughts, I pray;
See if there be some wicked way in me;
Cleanse me from every sin and set me free.

Proverbs 14:14 warns that the backslider in heart shall be filled with his own ways. Sometimes I wonder, who among us may not be with us in a year because they have failed to deal with what is in their hearts. In Matthew 15:8, Jesus said, "This people draweth nigh unto me with their mouth, and honoureth me with their lips; but their heart is far from me." We must ask ourselves the question,

"Have we learned to be a professional Pentecostal?"

What about our prayer life? Where is our devotion to God? Is our heart in our worship? Is it in the Word of God or are we just going through the motions? We must have a real, deep, strong, desire to be saved. What is in our hearts?

In Proverbs 4:23, "Keep thy heart with all diligence; for out of it are the issues of life." The devil would like for us to believe because we are tempted, we have sinned. This is not so. The Bible tells us in Hebrews 4:15, that Jesus was tempted in all points, like as we are, yet without sin.

Remember, all the water in the ocean cannot sink a ship. Only if the water gets inside the ship, will the ship sink. We are in this great, big ocean called the world, but we must not let the world into our hearts and sink our souls. Remember, what is in the well comes up in the bucket. What is in the heart will be revealed.

We must be careful of a self-righteous spirit and a "holier-than-thou" attitude. We are talking about the heart. In this next scripture, Jesus was dealing with the heart, with the spirit and with the thoughts.

> **Luke 18:9-14** <u>And he spake this parable unto certain which trusted in themselves that they were righteous, and despised others</u>: Two men went up into the temple to pray; the one a Pharisee, and the other a publican. The Pharisee stood and prayed thus with himself, God, I thank thee, that I am not as other men are, extortioners, unjust, adulterers, or even as this publican. I fast twice in the week, I give tithes of all that I possess. And the publican, standing afar off, would not lift up so much as his eyes unto heaven, but smote upon his breast, saying, God be merciful to me a sinner. I tell you; this man went down to his

house justified rather than the other: <u>for every one that exalteth himself shall be abased; and he that humbleth himself shall be exalted.</u>

We must not be as the people in Isaiah 65:5, "...Stand by thyself, come not near to me; for I am holier than thou. These are a smoke in my nose..." God hates a self-righteous, "holier-than-thou", "better-than-thou" attitude.

Matthew 23:25-28 Woe unto you, scribes and Pharisees, hypocrites! for ye make clean the outside of the cup and of the platter, <u>but within they are full of extortion and excess.</u> Thou blind Pharisee, cleanse first that which is within the cup and platter, that the outside of them may be clean also. Woe unto you, scribes and Pharisees, hypocrites! for ye are like unto whited sepulchres, which indeed appear beautiful outward, <u>but are within full of dead men's bones, and of all uncleanness.</u> Even so ye also outwardly appear righteous unto men, but within ye are full of hypocrisy and iniquity.

We can become unholy in our spirit. The opposite example of this hypocritical spirit is found in Psalms 51:17, "The sacrifices of God are a broken spirit: a broken and a contrite heart, O God, thou wilt not despise." This was the spirit of the humble publican who admitted his need for God's mercy. We must have a strong desire to be saved. We need an old-fashioned baptism of the fear of God!

Ecclesiastes 12:14 For God shall bring every work into judgment, with every secret thing, whether it be good, or whether it be evil.

Mark 7:20-23 And he said, That which cometh out of the man, that defileth the man. For from within, out of the heart of men, proceed evil thoughts, adulteries, fornications, murders, thefts, covetousness, wickedness, deceit, lasciviousness, an evil eye, blasphemy, pride, foolishness: <u>All these evil things come from within, and defile the man.</u>

We are talking about the heart. Remember what Jesus said in Mathew 5:28, "But I say unto you, that whosoever looketh on a woman to lust after her hath committed adultery with her already in his heart."

Hebrews 4:12 For the word of God is quick, and powerful, and sharper than any two-edged sword, piercing even to the dividing asunder of soul and spirit, and of the joints and marrow, and is a discerner of the thoughts and intents of the heart.

Ephesians 4:31-32 Let all bitterness, and wrath, and anger, and clamour, and evil speaking, be put away from you, with all malice: And be ye kind one to another, tenderhearted, forgiving one another, even as God for Christ's sake hath forgiven you.

Saints, we all need one another. I need somebody to watch for my soul. Backsliding or losing out with God is a process, and it starts from within. We must always be submitted to our God-given authority. We, including those of us in the ministry, must never come to the place that we cannot be talked to or dealt with, regardless of our position or age. We are instructed in I Peter 5:5, "Likewise, ye younger, submit yourselves unto the elder. Yea, all of you be subject one to another, and be clothed with humility: for God resisteth the proud, and giveth grace to the humble." The Bible also says in Hebrews 12:14-15, "Follow peace with all men, and holiness, without which no man shall see the Lord: Looking diligently lest any man fail of the grace of God; lest any root of bitterness springing up trouble you, and thereby many be defiled."

Our hope is found in verses 7 and 9 of I John chapter 1, "But if we walk in the light, as he is in the light, we have fellowship one with another, and the blood of Jesus Christ his Son cleanseth us from all sin… If we confess our sins, he is faithful and just to forgive us our sins, and to cleanse us from all unrighteousness."

Notice in verse 7 that the blood of Jesus Christ cleanseth us from ALL sin. The word *all* according to the Greek is "every sin, any sin or thoroughly." In the Hebrew, the word *all* is described as "complete and perfect." The definition of *all* in the dictionary is "totality and everything." The word *cleanseth* in the Greek means "to make clean and to purify." In Hebrew, it means "to make innocent or to make guiltless."

Read verse 9 again. If we will do ONE thing – JUST ONE THING - God will do four things for us. He will be faithful to us. He will be just with us. He will forgive us our sins. He will cleanse us from all unrighteousness.

> **2 Corinthians 7:1** Having therefore these promises, dearly beloved, let us cleanse ourselves from all filthiness of the flesh and spirit, perfecting holiness in the fear of God.

> **Jeremiah 4:14** O Jerusalem, wash thine heart from wickedness, that thou mayest be saved. How long shall thy vain thoughts lodge within thee?

Proverbs 30:12 There is a generation that are pure in their own eyes, and yet is not washed from their filthiness.

Phil. 4:8 Finally, brethren, whatsoever things are true, whatsoever things are honest, whatsoever things are just, whatsoever things are pure, whatsoever things are lovely, whatsoever things are of good report; if there be any virtue, and if there be any praise, think on these things.

Psalms 51:2, 10 Wash me throughly from mine iniquity, and cleanse me from my sin… Create in me a clean heart, O God; and renew a right spirit within me.

2 Chronicles 7:14 If my people, which are called by my name, shall humble themselves, and pray, and seek my face, and turn from their wicked ways; then will I hear from heaven, and will forgive their sin, and will heal their land.

We must ask ourselves, what are we becoming? Where are we going? Our most dominant thoughts will take us to where we are going, whether it be good, or it be bad. Thoughts become what we do. Thoughts become what we are. Thoughts become our life. We are the sum total of our thoughts. We will never be any better or higher than our best thoughts. For as a man thinketh in his heart so is he. Our thoughts control our life. We naturally gravitate toward that which we continually hold in our mind.

Psalms 94:11 The LORD knoweth the thoughts of man, that they are vanity.

I Chronicles 28:9 And thou, Solomon my son, know thou the God of thy father, and serve him with a perfect heart and with a willing mind: for the LORD searcheth all hearts, and understandeth all the imaginations of the thoughts: if thou seek him, he will be found of thee; but if thou forsake him, he will cast thee off for ever.

Mark 12:30 And thou shalt love the Lord thy God with all thy heart, and with all thy soul, and with all thy mind, and with all thy strength: this is the first commandment.

Hebrews 4:12 For the word of God is quick, and powerful, and sharper than any two-edged sword, piercing even to the dividing asunder of soul and spirit, and of the joints and marrow, and is a discerner of the thoughts and intents of the heart.

Psalms 139:23-24 Search me, O God, and know my heart: try me, and know my thoughts: And see if there be any wicked way in me, and lead me in the way everlasting.

Search me, O God, and know my heart today,

Try me, O Savior know my thoughts, I pray;

See if there be some wicked way in me;

Cleanse me from every sin and set me free.

I need Thee, Oh, I need Thee

Every hour I need thee;

Oh, bless me now, my Savior,

I come to Thee

WHAT SAITH THE SCRIPTURE?
Holiness of Speech

Ephesians 5:1-5 Be ye therefore followers of God, as dear children; 2 And walk in love, as Christ also hath loved us, and hath given himself for us an offering and a sacrifice to God for a sweetsmelling savour. 3 But fornication, and all uncleanness, or covetousness, let it not be once named among you, as becometh saints; 4 Neither filthiness, nor <u>foolish talking, nor jesting</u>, which are not convenient: but rather giving of thanks. 5 For this ye know, that no whoremonger, nor unclean person, nor covetous man, who is an idolater, hath any inheritance in the kingdom of Christ and of God.

What is the Apostle Paul telling us? He is saying that it is not fitting for us to use language, which is obscene, profane, or vulgar. Jesting here is intended to provoke laughter by using vulgar language. This would include filthy or suggestive talk and dirty stories. In verse 4, Paul uses the word *filthiness* which is telling us not to use obscene or filthy communication. We should not use dirty, vile, or foul talk.

Read verse 5 again. If someone starts that kind of talk, stop them or walk away. Do not be a partaker of that kind of talk.

Proverbs 4:23 Keep thy heart with all diligence; for out of it are the issues of life.

Matthew 12:34, 35 O generation of vipers, how can ye, being evil, speak good things? for out of the abundance of the heart the mouth speaketh. 35 A good man out of the good treasure of the heart bringeth forth good things: and an evil man out of the evil treasure bringeth forth evil things.

Proverbs 10:11 The mouth of a righteous man is a well of life: but violence covereth the mouth of the wicked.

Luke 6:43, 44 For a good tree bringeth not forth corrupt fruit; neither doth a corrupt tree bring forth good fruit. 44 For every tree is known by his own fruit. For of thorns men do not gather figs, nor of a bramble bush gather they grapes.

WHAT SAITH THE SCRIPTURE?
Holiness in Our Homes

Deuteronomy 7:26 <u>Neither shalt thou bring an abomination into thine house, lest thou be a cursed thing like it: but thou shalt utterly detest it, and thou shalt utterly abhor it; for it is a cursed thing.</u>

Psalms 101:3 <u>I will set no wicked thing before mine eyes:</u> I hate the work of them that turn aside; it shall not cleave to me.

Job 31:1 <u>I made a covenant with mine eyes;</u> why then should I think upon a maid?

Isaiah 33:15, 16 He that walketh righteously, and speaketh uprightly; he that despiseth the gain of oppressions, that shaketh his hands from holding of bribes, that stoppeth his ears from hearing of blood, <u>and shutteth his eyes</u>

from seeing evil; He shall dwell on high: his place of defence shall be the munitions of rocks: bread shall be given him; his waters shall be sure.

There was a tree set in the Garden of Eden that was called "The tree of the knowledge of good and evil." (Genesis 2:17) Adam was told to leave it alone. Television and other certain technologies have the knowledge of good and EVIL. To set these things before our eyes is to set EVIL before our eyes. Our entertainment has to do with our inward holiness. The children's song goes, "Oh! Be careful little eyes what you see."

Are we playing violent video games? What magazines and books are we reading? Do we idolize the world's sports heroes? What type of music and things are we listening to? **WHAT DOES JESUS THINK ABOUT THESE THINGS?**

If Jesus Came To Your House

by Lois Blanchard Eades

If Jesus came to your house to spend a day or two -
If He came unexpectedly, I wonder what you'd do.
Oh, I know you'd give your nicest room to such an honored Guest,
And all the food you'd serve to Him would be the very best,
And you would keep assuring Him you're glad to have Him there -
That serving Him in your own home is joy beyond compare.

But when you saw Him coming, would you meet Him at the door
With arms outstretched in welcome to your heavenly Visitor?
Or would you have to change your clothes before you let Him in?
Or hide some magazines and put the Bible where they'd been?
Would you turn off the radio and hope He hadn't heard?
And wish you hadn't uttered that last, loud, hasty word?

Would you hide your worldly music and put some hymn books out?
Could you let Jesus walk right in, or would you rush about?
And I wonder - if the Savior spent a day or two with you,
Would you go right on doing the things you always do?
Would you go right on saying the things you always say?
Would life for you continue as it does from day to day?

Would your family conversation keep up its usual pace?

And would you find it hard each meal to say a table grace?

Would you sing the songs you always sing, and read the books you read,

And let Him know the things on which your mind and spirit feed?

Would you take Jesus with you everywhere you'd planned to go?

Or would you, maybe, change your plans for just a day or so?

Would you be glad to have Him meet your very closest friends?

Or would you hope they'd stay away until His visit ends?

Would you be glad to have Him stay forever on and on?

Or would you sigh with great relief when He at last was gone?

It might be interesting to know the things that you would do

If Jesus Christ in person came to spend some time with you.

WHAT SAITH THE SCRIPTURE?
Outward Holiness

These things have to do with our outward holiness. This is not legalism. This is the scripture. People who love Jesus Christ do not have a problem with inward or outward holiness. When we know Him and love Him, it is not just our standard. It is our devotion to the Lord. If someone asks us about what we do and what we don't do, our response should be, "This is part of my devotion to God."

WHAT SAITH THE SCRIPTURE?
Holiness in Our Dress

Genesis 3:7 And the eyes of them both were opened, and they knew that they were naked; and they sewed fig leaves together, and made themselves aprons.

Genesis 3:21 Unto Adam also and to his wife did the LORD God make coats of skins, and clothed them.

God was not pleased with what Adam and Eve had made for themselves to wear as clothing. God clothed them the way He wanted them to dress. Our clothing reveals something of our spiritual condition. What we wear speaks for us.

Men and Women:

Exodus 28:2 And thou shalt make <u>holy garments</u> for Aaron thy brother for glory and for beauty.

Deuteronomy 22:5 The woman shall not wear that which pertaineth unto a man, neither shall a man put on a woman's garment: for all that do so are abomination unto the LORD thy God.

I Timothy 2:9 In like manner also, that women adorn themselves in modest apparel, with shamefacedness and sobriety; not with broided hair, or gold, or pearls, or costly array;

The word *modest* here in the Greek is translated as "of good behavior, proper and respectable." The dictionary defines *modesty* as "not showy, elaborate, or pretentious, not drawing attention."

Do our clothes fit too tightly and revealing? Our clothes should fit loosely and not reveal any part of our person. Are the dresses or skirts too short? A good rule to live by is the hem should be below the calf of the leg. Things keep getting shorter and shorter, but we want to take the safe route. Below the calf gives us a definite mark. Are there slits in the dresses and skirts? Wearing slits in dresses or skirts draws attention to the legs. Are the necklines too low? The neckline should be no lower than the collar bone. Are the sleeves too short? The sleeves should be past the elbow. Ladies, are the legs covered when in public? Our Apostolic ladies should wear nylons or tights when going out in public, especially when at the church. Wearing leggings is a step in the wrong direction.

Do the clothes we are wearing give us an alluring appearance or attitude? Some clothes display an attitude that is not becoming to a Christian. Remember, we are ambassadors in God's kingdom.

Talking about inward and outward holiness, it makes our hearts fear when we see, even among our Apostolics, men dressing and acting like a woman or women dressing and acting like a "toughie." As mentioned above in Deuteronomy 22:5, God has always made a sharp difference in the dress and actions of men as compared to women. Feminine clothing on men and pants on women is still out of style with God. Men ought to wear pants and women ought to wear dresses or skirts. Ladies, what are you wearing to go snow skiing or water skiing? What are you wearing at home?

May God fill our hearts with the Holy Ghost until the men want to be men and the women want to be women, in spirit and in dress. "Unisex" tendencies and homosexual styles in any form, among men or women, are not holiness.

> **Zephaniah 1:8** And it shall come to pass in the day of the LORD'S sacrifice, that I will punish the princes, and the king's children, and all such as <u>are clothed with strange apparel.</u>

The Hebrew translation for *strange* is "foreign, different, alien, outlandish, or adulterous." The king's children were not dressed according to the way God's people dressed. They had adopted the dress of the sinner's apparel or the foreigner's apparel. We, the children of the King of Kings, need not to adopt the dress of the world.

WHAT SAITH THE SCRIPTURE?
Makeup

There are examples showing us that makeup was a mark of the heathen women and unfaithful women throughout the Bible. The face has much to say about the person's character and experience.

I Corinthians 10:5, 6 But with many of them God was not well pleased: for they were overthrown in the wilderness. <u>Now these things were our examples, to the intent we should not lust after evil things, as they also lusted.</u>

1 Corinthians 10:11 <u>Now all these things happened unto them for ensamples: and they are written for our admonition,</u> upon whom the ends of the world are come.

2 Kings 9:30 And when Jehu was come to Jezreel, Jezebel heard of it; and <u>she painted her face</u>, and tired her head, and looked out at a window.

Ezekiel 23:40 And furthermore, that ye have sent for men to come from far, unto whom a messenger was sent; and, lo, they came: for whom thou didst wash thyself, <u>paintedst thy eyes, and deckedst thyself with ornaments,</u>

Jeremiah 4:30 And when thou art spoiled, what wilt thou do? <u>Though thou clothest thyself with crimson, though thou deckest thee with ornaments of gold, though thou rentest thy face with painting, in vain shalt thou make thyself fair</u>; thy lovers will despise thee, they will seek thy life.

I Timothy 2:9 In like manner also, that women adorn themselves in modest apparel, with <u>shamefacedness</u> and sobriety; not with broided hair, or gold, or pearls, or costly array;

Shamefacedness, from the Greek, portrays modesty and bashfulness. Anything or any item that we add (to our face) that is fake would be considered makeup. Thank God that our true Apostolics are still cleansing themselves from makeup, regardless of worldly trends such as foundation, blush, eyeshadow, eyeliner, mascara, eyebrow pencil, false eyelashes, lipstick, lip gloss, spray tan, fake fingernails, fake toenails, and such like. God is still beautifying the meek with salvation. Painted fingernails or toenails, clear or color, is still out of style with true holiness people.

WHAT SAITH THE SCRIPTURE?
Hair

Dying of the Hair:

Proverbs 20:29 The glory of young men is their strength: and the <u>beauty of old men is the gray head.</u>

Proverbs 16:31 The <u>hoary (means gray or white) head</u> is a crown of glory, if it be found in the way of righteousness.

Gray hair on a Christian is a symbol of beauty and honor. Dying the hair, bleaching, tinting or "such like" should not be found among us.

Revelation 1:14 His head and his hairs were white like wool, as white as snow; and his eyes were as a flame of fire…

I Samuel 12:2 And now, behold, the king walketh before you: and I am old and grayheaded; and, behold, my sons are with you: and I have walked before you from my childhood unto this day.

Job 15:10 With us are both the grayheaded and very aged men, much elder than thy father.

It is evident through the scriptures that gray hair is a crown of glory for a righteous saint of God. Even the Lord, in the book of Revelation, has hair white as snow. We should not alter or change the color of our hair.

Men's Hair:

Ezekiel 44:20 Neither shall they shave their heads, nor suffer their locks to grow long; they shall only poll their heads.

I Corinthians 11:3-4, 7, 14 But I would have you know, that the head of every man is Christ; and the head of the woman is the man; and the head of Christ is God. 4 Every man praying or prophesying, having his head covered, dishonoureth his head. ... 7 For a man indeed ought not to cover his head, forasmuch as he is the image and glory of God: but the woman is the glory of the man. ... 14 <u>Doth not even nature itself teach you, that, if a man have long hair, it is a shame unto him?</u>

The word *shame* in the Greek means, "dishonor, ignominy, disgrace, infamy, reproach, or vile." Short hair on a man is a symbol of his authority in the home and his obedience to God's

Word. Long hair on a man is a symbol of his rebellion against God.

Throughout all of history, facial hair on men has represented many different things. Not all of it has been good. In today's time and culture, it is no different. One of the simple ways for our men to represent the new "clean" life is to be clean-shaven. It is very common that a man, who has been born again and is sensitive to the Holy Ghost, gets a conviction to shave his facial hair on his own.

Women's Hair:

I Corinthians 11:5-15 But every woman that prayeth or prophesieth with her head uncovered dishonoureth her head: for that is even all one as if she were shaven. 6 For if the woman be not covered, let her also be shorn: but if it be a shame for a woman to be shorn or shaven, let her be covered. 7 For a man indeed ought not to cover his head, forasmuch as he is the image and glory of God: but the woman is the glory of the man. 8 For the man is not of the woman; but the woman of the man. 9 Neither was the man created for the woman; but the woman for the man. 10 For this cause ought the woman to have power on her head because of the angels. 11 Nevertheless neither is the man without the woman, neither the woman without the man, in the Lord. 12 For as the woman is of the man, even so is the man also by the woman; but all things of God. 13 Judge in yourselves: is it comely that a woman pray unto God uncovered? 14 Doth not even nature itself teach you, that, if a man have long hair, it is a shame unto him? 15 <u>But if a woman have long hair, it is a glory to her: for her hair is given her for a covering.</u>

Long hair on a woman is a symbol of her submission to man's authority and her obedience to God's Word. The scripture tells us if she cuts her hair, she dishonors man and her authority. It brings shame to her and disregards the angels. She loses her power and glory. Ultimately, she is disobeying the Word of God. This also means that our little Pentecostal girls' hair should never be cut!

WHAT SAITH THE SCRIPTURE?
Jewelry

I Timothy 2:8, 9 I will therefore that men pray every where, <u>lifting up holy hands</u>, without wrath and doubting. In like manner also, that women adorn themselves in modest apparel, with shamefacedness and sobriety; not with broided hair, <u>or gold, or pearls, or costly array;</u>

I Peter 3:3 Whose adorning let it not be that outward adorning of plaiting the hair, and of <u>wearing of gold</u>, or of putting on of apparel;

Let it not be the outward adorning. The word *adorning* in the Greek means "decoration." The dictionary's definition is "to decorate with ornaments."

God's people have a powerful inward beauty. They do not need any of the above ornamentations, nor do they need jewelry. Jewelry includes bracelets, necklaces, brooches, earrings, cufflinks, tie clasps, tie pins, watches that look like bracelets, or various ornaments for the hair, face or body. Also included are rings such as friendship rings, birthstone rings, class rings, engagement rings, wedding rings, and any ring that you put on your fingers or toes.

Someone asked one of our old elders where he got his scriptures about wearing rings. He said, "I use the same scriptures you use for <u>earrings</u>."

Exodus 35:21, 22 And they came, every one whose heart stirred him up, and every one whom his spirit made willing, and they brought the LORD'S offering to the work of the tabernacle of the congregation, and for all his service, and for the holy garments. And they came, both men and women, as many as were willing hearted, <u>and brought bracelets, and earrings, and rings, and tablets, all jewels of gold:</u> and every man that offered offered an offering of gold unto the LORD.

The jewelry mentioned in these verses is what the Israelites brought out of Egypt. Egypt represents the world of sin. When God delivered the Israelites from the bondage of Egypt (the world), God's people gave up the jewelry for the building of the tabernacle.

Jeremiah 4:30 And when thou art spoiled, what wilt thou do? Though thou clothest thyself with crimson, <u>though thou deckest thee with ornaments of gold,</u> though thou rentest thy face with painting, in vain shalt thou make thyself fair; thy lovers will despise thee, they will seek thy life.

Isaiah 3:16-26 Moreover the LORD saith, Because the daughters of Zion are haughty, and walk with stretched forth necks and wanton eyes, walking and mincing as they go, and making a tinkling with their feet: Therefore the Lord will smite with a scab the crown of the head of the daughters of Zion, and the LORD will discover their secret parts. In that day the Lord will take away the bravery of their tinkling ornaments about their feet, and their cauls, and their round tires like the moon, The chains, and the bracelets, and the mufflers, The bonnets, and the ornaments of the legs, and the headbands, and the tablets, and the earrings, The rings, and nose jewels, The changeable suits of apparel, and the mantles, and the wimples, and the crisping pins, The glasses, and the fine linen, and the hoods, and the vails. And it shall come to pass, [that] instead of sweet smell there shall be stink; and instead of a girdle a rent; and instead of well set hair baldness; and instead of a stomacher a girding of sackcloth; [and] burning instead of beauty. Thy men shall fall by the sword, and thy mighty in the war. And her gates shall lament and mourn; and she [being] desolate shall sit upon the ground.

The prophets Jeremiah and Isaiah tell us of the attitude connected to jewelry and ornamentation. The end result in both passages is defeat.

WHAT SAITH THE SCRIPTURE?
Separation

The doctrine of separation from the world as found in the scriptures:

Leviticus 20:24, 26 But I have said unto you, Ye shall inherit their land, and I will give it unto you to possess it, a land that floweth with milk and honey: <u>I am the LORD your God, which have separated you from other people. And ye shall be holy unto me</u>: for I the LORD am holy, <u>and have severed you from other people, that ye should be mine</u>.

Ezra 9:1 Now when these things were done, the princes came to me, saying, The people of Israel, and the priests, and the Levites, have not <u>separated themselves from the people of the lands</u>...

2 Corinthians 6:14 Be ye not unequally yoked together with unbelievers: for what fellowship hath righteousness with unrighteousness? and what communion hath light with darkness?

2 Corinthians 6:17 Wherefore come out from among them, <u>and be ye separate, saith the Lord,</u> and touch not the unclean thing; and I will receive you,

John 15:19 If ye were of the world, the world would love his own: but because ye are not of the world, but I have chosen you out of the world, therefore the world hateth you.

I John 2:15 Love not the world, neither the things that are in the world. If any man love the world, the love of the Father is not in him.

I John 2:16 For all that is in the world, the lust of the flesh, and the lust of the eyes, and the pride of life, is not of the Father, but is of the world.

I John 2:17 And the world passeth away, and the lust thereof: but he that doeth the will of God abideth for ever.

Matthew 7:13, 14 Enter ye in at the strait gate: for wide is the gate, and broad is the way, that leadeth to destruction, and many there be which go in thereat: Because strait is the gate, and narrow is the way, which leadeth unto life, and few there be that find it.

The song says, "The good ol' Bible's right Hallelujah to the Lamb!"

Separation from the world is the will of God. When we talk about separation from the world, we are not talking about separating ourselves in the sense that we become an ineffective witness. It is the will of God for us to reach the world. We are in the world but not of the world.

John instructs us in I John 2:15, "Love not the world, neither the things that are in the world." One of the signs of the end time, mentioned by Paul in II Timothy 3:4, is that people will be lovers of pleasure more than lovers of God. We must be careful and keep ourselves properly separated from the spirit of the world because the spirit of this world is not the spirit of holiness.

The pool hall, bowling alleys, arcades, skating rinks, movie theaters, etc. – there is something about these places that have the spirit of the world. They pull away from holiness. We also need to separate ourselves from worldly sports, going to ball games, little league, big league, church league, city league, and Christian school tournaments. We don't need any of them. This does not mean that we are against activities. I think we can all agree that our young people need activities, but not the kind of activities that mixes us with the world or puts us in competition to the place that the "spirit of sports" takes hold of us. This kind of spirit generates the spirit of the world. Sports have become America's latest form of idolatry, such as keeping up with what team is playing what team, and who's the best quarterback or pitcher in the league, etc. This type of activity and interest leads to watching the games in some manner, going to the games and preoccupation with vanities which lead to no good.

WHAT SAITH THE SCRIPTURE?
In Conclusion

In closing, we are Christians. Being Christ-like is our measuring stick. When it comes to holiness within and holiness without and separation from the world, a good rule to live by is to ask ourselves, "What would Jesus say?" What would He say concerning inward and outward holiness and separation from the world? The safe route is always the best route. It is a privilege for us to be on this highway of holiness. Remember, holiness is the Christian way of life.

The world and the unholy spirit of the world are always trying to creep in. We must be diligent.

Psalms 101:2, 3 I will behave myself wisely in a perfect way. O when wilt thou come unto me? I will walk within my house with a perfect heart. I will set no wicked thing before mine eyes: I hate the work of them that turn aside; [it] shall not cleave to me.

I Peter 1:16 Because it is written, Be ye holy; for I am holy.

Note to the Preacher

We preachers need to keep praying and preaching. If we are not careful, we can become weary in well-doing. We must not become weary when it comes to holiness preaching and teaching. In II Timothy 3:1-2 we read, "This know also, that in the last days perilous times shall come. For men shall be lovers of their own selves, covetous, boasters, proud, blasphemers, disobedient to parents, unthankful, unholy..." According to this scripture, one of the signs of the last days is men would be unholy. I thank God that in these last days there is a people that are not partakers of the unholy spirit of the end time. God is still calling His people to holiness even in these last days. Ephesians 5:27 states, "That he might present it to himself a glorious church, not having spot, or wrinkle, or any such thing; but that it should <u>be holy and without blemish</u>."

P.S. - Let our preaching be with all wisdom and grace in the right spirit, at the right time, and in the right way.

CPSIA information can be obtained
at www.ICGtesting.com
Printed in the USA
LVHW012014151019
634130LV00019B/7804/P

ISBN 9781695927452

90 000

9 781695 927452